BRINGING UP GIRLS
BIBLE STUDY

SHAPING THE NEXT GENERATION OF WOMEN

DR. JAMES DOBSON

developed with Nic Allen

LifeWay Press®
Nashville, Tennessee

Published by LifeWay Press®
© 2014 Siggie, LLC

Bringing Up Girls © 2014 by Dr. James Dobson. Published by Tyndale House Publishers;
Carol Stream, IL. Used by Permission.

ISBN: 978-1-4300-3303-5
Item: 005650365

Dewey decimal classification: 649
Subject headings: CHILD REARING \ GIRLS \ WOMEN

All Scripture quotations are taken from the Holman Christian Standard Bible. Copyright © 1999,
2000, 2002, 2003, 2009 by Holman Bible Publishers. Used by permission. Holman Christian Standard
Bible® and HCSB® are federally registered trademarks of Holman Bible Publishers.
Cover Photo: Randy Hughes/LifeWay Photo.

To order additional copies of this resource, write to LifeWay Church Resources, Customer Service,
One LifeWay Plaza, Nashville, TN 37234-0113; fax 615.251.5933; phone 800.458.2772; order online
at *www.lifeway.com* or email *orderentry@lifeway.com;* or visit the LifeWay Christian Store serving you.

Printed in the United States of America

Adult Ministry Publishing, LifeWay Church Resources, One LifeWay Plaza, Nashville, TN 37234-0152

Contents

About the Author

DR. JAMES DOBSON is the founder and president of Family Talk, a non-profit organization that produces his radio program, "Dr. James Dobson's Family Talk." He is the author of more than 50 books dedicated to the preservation of the family, including *The New Dare to Discipline; Love for a Lifetime; Life on the Edge; Love Must Be Tough; The New Strong-Willed Child; When God Doesn't Make Sense; Bringing Up Boys; Bringing Up Girls; Head Over Heels;* and, most recently, *Dr. Dobson's Handbook of Family Advice.*

Dr. Dobson served as an associate clinical professor of pediatrics at the University of Southern California School of Medicine for fourteen years and on the attending staff of Children's Hospital of Los Angeles for seventeen years in the divisions of Child Development and Medical Genetics. He has been active in governmental affairs and has advised three U.S. presidents on family matters.

He earned his PhD from the University of Southern California (1967) in child development and holds eighteen honorary doctoral degrees. He was inducted in 2009 into the National Radio Hall of Fame.

Dr. Dobson and his wife, Shirley, reside in Colorado Springs, Colorado. They have two grown children, Danae and Ryan, and two grandchildren.

NIC ALLEN helped with the curriculum development of this study. After spending ten years in student ministry, Nic became the family and children's pastor at Rolling Hills Community Church in Franklin, Tennessee. Nic has written for several LifeWay Bible studies, including *Courageous, Facing the Giants,* and *Flywheel.* Nic and his wife, Susan, have three children: Lillie Cate, Nora Blake, and Simon.

How to Use This Study

The four sessions of this study may be used weekly or during a weekend retreat. But we recommend that before you dig into this material, you watch the film, *Bringing Up Girls* from the *Dr. James Dobson Presents: Building a Family Legacy* film series. This will lay the groundwork for your study.

This material has been written for a small-group experience, for you and your spouse, or for personal study.

An option to extend or conclude this study is for your group to view the film *Your Legacy* from the *Dr. James Dobson Presents: Building a Family Legacy* film series.

CONNECT: The purpose of the introductory section of each session invites and motivates you to connect with the topic of the session and others in your group.

WATCH: The study DVD contains four DVD clips which include introductions from Ryan Dobson and clips from a talk by Dr. James Dobson, based on the film and the accompanying book *Bringing Up Girls* by Dr. Dobson (Tyndale Momentum; ISBN 978-1-4143-9132-8.)

ENGAGE: This section is the primary focus of each week's group time. You and the other participants will further engage the truths of Scripture and discuss accompanying questions. This section will also include a Wrap Up portion, which concludes the group session and leads to the Reflect section.

REFLECT: This at-home study section helps you dig deeper into Scripture and apply the truths you're learning. Go deeper each week by reading the suggested chapters in the book *Bringing Up Girls* and completing the activities at the end of each session in this study.

Guidelines for Groups

While you can complete this study alone, you will benefit greatly from covering the material with your spouse or with the interaction of a Sunday school class or small group. Here are a few ways to cultivate a valuable experience as you engage in this study.

PREPARATION: To get the most out of each group time, read through the study each week and answer the questions so you're ready to discuss the material. It will also be helpful for you and your group members to have copies of the book *Bringing Up Girls* (ISBN 978-1-4143-9132-8). Read it in advance of the study to prepare, and encourage your members to read the corresponding chapters each week. In your group, don't let one or two people shoulder the entire responsibility for conversation and participation. Everyone can pitch in and contribute.

CONFIDENTIALITY: In the study, you will be prompted to share thoughts, feelings, and personal experiences. Accept others where they are without judgment. Many of the challenges discussed will be private. These should be kept in strict confidence by the group.

RESPECT: Participants must respect each other's thoughts and opinions, providing a safe place for those insights to be shared without fear of judgment or unsolicited advice (including hints, sermons, instructions, and scriptural Band-Aids®). Take off your fix-it hat and leave it at the door, so you can just listen. If advice is requested, then it's okay to lend your opinion, seasoned with grace and offered with love.

ACCOUNTABILITY: Each week, participants will be challenged in their intentional parenting of their daughters. Commit to supporting and encouraging each other during the sessions and praying for each other between meetings.

Introduction

You have a daughter. Maybe more than one.

From the moment you first heard, "It's a girl"—whether in an ultrasound room after twenty weeks of curiosity, in a delivery room after nine months of waiting, or after receiving the news of a successful adoption—you have been dreaming about the life your girl will lead.

Wife? Mom? Missionary? Valedictorian? Social leader? Artist? Athlete? Techie? Scientist? Writer?

The options are endless. In eras past, women's careers were often limited. Not so anymore. Now girls have their pick of options in jobs, schools, and sports. But for parents of girls, future vocations are not their only concerns. There are the powerful influences of the media, friends, and a culture that sometimes presses your daughter toward behaviors that are in conflict with what you believe. Things like:

- Eating disorders
- Body mutilation
- Sexually transmitted diseases
- Unwed pregnancy
- Homosexuality
- Bullying
- Binge drinking

As you parent your daughter, it's easy to settle for status quo in order to sidestep really big problems. Dreaming with your girl about being a vocalist or veterinarian takes a backseat to making sure she doesn't contract an STD or experiment with drugs.

Simply protecting your daughter from falling into serious trouble isn't the primary goal. Instead of focusing on what you don't want, focus on what you do want. Your ultimate goal as her parent involves intentional participation as she builds godly character.

And isn't that what you are praying for? It doesn't matter if she's a soccer mom or the CEO of a major corporation. The important questions are: Does she love Jesus? Does she have strong character and integrity? Is she modest? Is she an encourager? Does she respect herself, authority, and other people?

These attitudes are not automatic. The culture emphasizes altogether different values for women, oversexualizing and demoralizing them. The media promote the world's agenda, overturning your good efforts. These qualities must be intentionally taught. And cultivated. This challenge can't be won alone. You need the Lord to give you patience and empower your efforts and your daughter's response to developing into a Christ-honoring woman. And you need encouragement from other parents who have set similar goals.

The aim of this study is to motivate and instruct you as a mom or dad to help encourage your daughter toward completeness in Christ.

Of course, this "Bringing Up Girls" experience will not guarantee perfect parenting; it simply offers an environment for growth in a small group with other parents of girls. Accompanied by a weekly personal reflection section to engage the Bible on your own, this study is designed to equip you with questions to consider, steps to take, and passages from God's Word to inspire and guide you.

And don't underestimate the impact of examining the Scriptures together. The Bible calls this experience of brothers and sisters working together for a common goal, "His body ... the church." And God's promise is that when you gather, He will join you. The Holy Spirit will be a member of your group. Around your circle, He will give wisdom. He may speak to you through the others gathered, or He may quietly whisper to you with His "still, small voice."

As you engage this study, may God richly reward your effort and radically bless your family. And may your daughter's life forever be impacted for good by this experience.

WEEK 1

THE WONDERFULLY DIFFERENT WORLD OF GIRLS

· · · · · · · · · · · ·

BEFORE YOU BEGIN, take time to pray with your group. Ask God to teach the group how to be proactive, loving parents to their children just as He is to us.

It's no surprise that girls and boys are different. For years, activists have attempted to homogenize our understanding of boys and girls, attributing the differences between the sexes to paternalistic biases in upbringing. Physiologically, brain scans proved the truth and eventually many doctors and sociologists had to agree: boys and girls really are different.

From your observation, what are the differences between boys and girls?

What is your biggest goal or dream for your daughter at this stage in her life?

What are you praying for right now in your daughter's life?

Is there a particular challenge that she's facing that you could be praying about?

What question do you hope this study will address?

WATCH CLIP 1 from the study DVD and answer the following questions:

What struck you as the most urgent reason to focus on how we raise girls?

FOR DADS: Respond to this statement: "There's an assault on self-worth among girls today." What is the father's role in influencing a daughter's self-esteem?

FOR MOMS: Describe your relationship with your own father. How has it affected your life?

The clip identified some key social concerns: binge drinking, anorexia, bulimia, cutting, abortion, and sexual aggressiveness, to name a few. Have you ever discussed these topics with your daughter to gauge her exposure to them and her thoughts about them? Why would it be a good idea to have that conversation?

How will you intentionally get in touch with what's going on in her world?

CONTINUE YOUR GROUP TIME with this discussion guide.

God's Word has ample wisdom for parenting. As we examine passages of Scripture, consider the following: a) what the words meant to the original audience, b) what they mean to all believers for all time, and c) what the passage means for us today as the parents of a daughter.

Let's start at the beginning.

> So God created man in His own image;
> He created him in the image of God;
> He created them male and female.
> **GENESIS 1:27**

Eve was essential to God's creation from the very beginning. The first chapter of the Bible includes a woman as an integral part of God's image reflected in humanity.

How does the uniqueness of women reflect the image and character of God?

How is the character of God reflected in your daughter?

READ Genesis 2:18-24.

These details add additional context for the creation of humankind. In Genesis 1, God declared each part of His creation good. Genesis 2 reveals how God knew that something in creation was not good: man was alone. Something was missing: woman. In her, creation became complete.

Adam was formed from dust. Eve was fashioned from Adam. From the very beginning, this special relationship between men and women has defined God's intention for His creation.

> **How do you see God's design being rejected? How are girls becoming victims because of this?**

In a study I conducted that's explained in my book, *What Wives Wish Their Husbands Knew about Women,* the most frequent source of depression among young women was low self-esteem, far exceeding any other cause. More than 50 percent listed low self-esteem in first place, and 80 percent marked it in the top five. The women who served as the test group were young, attractive, and married. All were mothers with young children and lived in middle-class neighborhoods. Most had college degrees and were church members. Nevertheless, almost all of them reportedly dealt with recurring bouts of depression and flagging confidence.[1]

> **How might their sense of inadequacy play out in these women's marriages? In their parenting? In their friendships?**

READ Genesis 3:16.

> **What link do you see between God's punishment and the research presented above?**

Results of the sin of Adam and Eve are still in effect today. It's not so much that a woman longs for a man who in turn rules over her, but that she longs for a human connection that makes her feel valued and delighted in. The curse of sin damaged the trusting camaraderie between women and men that hasn't been replaced.

Women, when do you feel delighted in and valued?

Men, how has meeting this need in your wife and daughter been modeled for you?

How can you value and delight in your daughter, helping her see she is lovely and necessary and that, in her femininity, God's creation was complete?

Women have a core need to know that they are loved and that they are lovely. If your daughter doesn't get that foundation of self-worth and appreciation at home, she could spend the rest of her life searching for it from other, less healthy sources. Your ongoing message needs to be that she is beautiful inside and out to you and to her Creator. Your goal is to help her set high standards, encouraging her to make friends (and a spouse) who support that affirming view of who she is.

READ Ephesians 2:1 and 4:22-24.

There is a war going on in your child's heart. The world wants your daughter to see herself as the world sees her. God wants your daughter to take on a new self that represents His righteousness and truth.

How is the newness of Christ evident in your life? In the life of your daughter?

Name three ways the world is battling for control of your daughter's heart. What can you do about one of them this week?

THIS WEEK'S INSIGHTS

- Our daughters are unique. Their femininity is a special part of creation that bears the image of God.
- Our daughters' deepest desire is to know that they are loved and are lovely.
- There is a war going on for the rights to our daughters' hearts. God wants to restore His image in her life through the life and likeness of His Son. The world wants to tell her that her worth is found in possessions, looks, and others' opinions.

How can you convey these important truths to your daughter this week?

How can you embrace these truths for yourself?

WRAP UP

PRAY TOGETHER asking God to grow your daughters into the image bearer He desires them to be.

> Lord, empower us to be good stewards of the
> treasures You have given us in our daughters. Help
> us steer them toward becoming the image bearers
> You desire them to be. Give us wisdom, patience, and
> strength in this journey. Grant them open hearts to
> hear You speak and willing spirits to obey. Amen.

READ AND COMPLETE the activities for this section before your next group time. For further insight, read chapters 1 and 4 from the book *Bringing Up Girls.*

> "When our girls were young, we celebrated parent/child dedication in our church. One of the things we did was to choose a life verse for each of our daughters. We pray their verses over them often and even painted each verse on a canvas for their room. Those verses have become mission statements for how we raise them."
> **SUSAN, *mother of two girls***

FOUR STEPS FOR PARENTS

Before we launch into the four primary components for bringing up godly girls, let's let Scripture put everything in perspective.

READ DEUTERONOMY 6:4-9.

For Jews, this passage is referred to as the Shema. It was a declaration of faith in God and part of a daily prayer ritual. Jesus quoted these words when asked to condense God's law to the most important command. Verse 5, "Love the LORD your God with all your heart, with all your soul, and with all your strength," is the mission statement for a believer, and verses 6 through 9 are the step-by-step instructions for accomplishing that mission and passing it on to the next generation.

Do you have a life verse or personal mission statement? If so, write it here.

Now take time to consider a mission statement for your daughter. Write it here.

Children need a constant reminder and understanding of who God is and what He expects from them. Moses takes that responsibility a step further in Deuteronomy 6. He tells parents to talk about spiritual matters continually. Notice that Moses didn't just make a suggestion to parents about the spiritual training of the children. He called that assignment a "commandment." It's not enough to mutter, "Now I lay me down to sleep" with your exhausted child at the end of the day. Instead, there is urgency in Moses' words.

As parents, we have four steps in bringing up godly girls.

1. TALK TO YOUR CHILDREN ABOUT THE LORD AND HIS MERCIES CONTINUALLY. This is what Moses told the children of Israel. It's also what King David and the prophet Joel, among other biblical authors, instructed us to do. These passages are too clear to be misunderstood.

Read the following verses and briefly record your takeaways from each.

Psalm 34:11:

Psalm 78:4-6:

Psalm 145:4:

Joel 1:3:

Take advantage of every opportunity to tell your children that faith in God is pivotal in life, as is His love for them. Begin this introduction to spiritual truths when your children are very young.

2. **TEACH YOUR CHILDREN TO PRAY AS EARLY AS POSSIBLE.** My parents, grandparents and even great grandparents took that responsibility very seriously. I began trying to pray even before I learned to talk. I had heard my parents praying during their private devotions, and I began imitating the sounds they made. My mother and father were shocked and wondered how that was possible for a child at thirteen months of age. Remember, your children are observing you and are influenced by everything you do.

3. **TEACH YOUR CHILDREN THE IMPORTANCE OF STUDYING AND MEMORIZING SCRIPTURE.** Psalm 119:11 reads, "I have treasured Your word in my heart so that I may not sin against You." If you want your children to be guided morally when they are beyond your reach, begin teaching them the importance of Scripture when they are young. It's amazing how often a relevant biblical reference comes to mind when wisdom and discernment are required. If those verses have not been "downloaded" to our brains, we will have to figure out what to do based on our own limited understanding.

4. **PRAY FOR YOUR DAUGHTER CONTINUALLY.** Prayer is one of God's most mysterious and remarkable gifts to us. It's our lifeline to the most holy of relationships, our opportunity to directly express our praises and desires to the Creator of the universe. There is power in this simple act that can't fully be explained, yet can never be denied. And it's our most effective means of investing in the welfare of our children.

PRECIOUS GIFT

Your daughter is a treasure to you. Take a few moments to recall and record your thoughts and feelings of when you held her for the first time.

When your daughter was born, what dreams did you have for her?

What fears did you have?

Go to a quiet place and read aloud Psalm 139.

Now read the passage aloud again, this time substituting the name of your daughter each time it says "me," "my," or "I." For example, verse 1 might read, "You have searched my daughter 'Anna' and know her." If you have more than one daughter, take time to repeat this passage in its entirety for each of your girls.

How does reading this passage with your daughter in mind affect your view of her and your responsibility in raising her?

How does realizing that the God of the universe knows her and holds her close ease your fears?

Without their parents to protect and defend them, girls are on their own against formidable forces. The influence that parents wield for good or harm in their daughters' lives touches every dimension of life, shaping and stabilizing girls' sense of worth and buoying their tender spirits. Hug her. Compliment her admirable traits. Build her confidence by giving her your time and attention. Defend her when she is struggling. And let her know that she has a place in your heart that is reserved for only her. She will never forget it.

Remember that your children are yours to nurture. God created your daughter in His image and gave her to you to raise as His image bearer. It's a wonderful blessing and an enormous responsibility—one you can't perform perfectly or on your own. Ask for His wisdom and guidance to shape your parenting.

PERSONAL REFLECTION

Spend some time this week reflecting on the following questions.

What/who do you currently regard as the biggest threat to God's image in your daughter?

What is your plan for protecting and defending your daughter against that formidable force?

1. James Dobson, *What Wives Wish Their Husbands Knew About Women* (Carol Stream, Illinois: Tyndale Publishers, Inc., 2003), 22.

WEEK 2

THE WOEFULLY DAMAGING EFFECTS OF CULTURE

START YOUR GROUP TIME by discussing what participants discovered in their Reflect homework.

Now let's dive into the damaging effects of culture. What does culture value? Consider some article titles from the checkout line:

- "30 Things to Do With a Naked Man" (*Cosmo*, 2012)
- "4 Questions About Emergency Contraception" (*Self*, 2012)
- "Nice Butt! 21 Tricks for a Bikini-Ready Booty" (*Allure*, 2012)
- "13 Signs You're Ready to Move in Together" (*Glamour*, 2012)

What do all of these messages have in common?

What article titles would you like your daughter to read instead? Brainstorm a few.

But magazines aren't the only culprits. Television, movies, music, the Internet, and social media all contribute to moral decline in our society.

What are the most damaging messages women receive from popular media and culture today? How is that message communicated to young girls?

How did popular culture and peer pressure play a part in your story as a preteen or teen?

WATCH CLIP 2 from the study DVD and answer the following questions:

A father's presence in a daughter's life is very important. What are some ways he can safeguard values of modesty and purity for his daughter?

On a scale of 1-10, do you consider yourself to be clueless or aware when it comes to the cultural influences warring against healthy ideals?

1	2	3	4	5	6	7	8	9	10
Clueless									Aware

Which of the following best describes your family's current response to culture? Why?
☐ Fully embrace
☐ Underestimate the damage
☐ Shrink and hide
☐ Prayerfully and biblically combat

There are many things that can give culture the upper hand. Where are you on the following continuum?

Asleep at the Wheel   Rested and Ready

CONTINUE YOUR GROUP TIME with this discussion guide.

Before we examine what Scripture says about culture's influence on our daughters, let's discuss some of the following statistics facing today's families and girls:

- Half of all first marriages will end in divorce.
- 40 percent of children in the U.S. go to bed each night without a biological father in their home.
- 30 percent of Americans say drinking is a problem in their home.
- Sex is the number one searched-for term on the Internet today.
- Two out of every three shows on TV contain sexual content.
- The number one wish for girls ages 11–17 is to be thinner.
- Nationwide, 46 percent of students in grades 9–12 have had sex.
- 14 percent of all 13-year-olds have had sex.
- Nearly 35 percent of all young women become pregnant at least once before reaching the age of 20—almost 850,000 each year.
- Approximately 1.5 million U.S. women with unwanted pregnancies choose abortion each year.
- 83 percent of teens say that moral truth depends on the situation.[1]

Which statistic is most alarming to you? Why?

In what way(s) do you attempt to guard and protect your daughter from the negative influences of culture and the harmful effects they cause?

It's so easy to drift along in the powerful stream of culture, wanting the things the world tells us to want and being motivated by things far from God. Even as believers, we sometimes find ourselves longing for what culture says is worthwhile. The following passages of Scripture give us important instructions concerning culture.

READ Hebrews 2:1.

To not drift away, we can focus on the message of Jesus.

> What does it mean to focus on the message of Jesus?
> Does it mean doing more—more serving activities and
> more commanding your mind to obey and feel joy?
> If not, then what does it mean?

> How can you display your understanding of Jesus
> in your home?

READ Psalm 73:16-17.

The first half of Psalm 73 exposes the heart of a man who is envious
of evil people and how they seem to prosper despite their wickedness.
The latter half reveals the heart of another who is reminded of the true
destiny of the wicked and his true place in God's presence. Verses 16
and 17 provide the turning point. To have God's perspective, we need
to know what it means to actually experience the presence of God.

> What are ways that you can experience
> God's presence?

> What effect does/would His companionship
> have on you?

> Does your daughter observe you experiencing
> God's presence? Give examples.

What questions should we be asking our girls concerning the presence of God in their lives?

It's important to understand how your daughter sees God. If she sees Him as demanding, distant, or disinterested in her hopes, hurts, and heart, then no amount of brilliant, anti-cultural instruction will matter. But if she has met a compassionate, forgiving God—One who wept at Lazarus' death and rejoices when He sees the prodigal come home—then she has a pliable foundation for absorbing His insights on the wise way to live.

Remember that you don't need more willpower to stand up to culture; you need an understanding of the power of repentance and restoration. You need Someone who loves you and wants His best for you. Someone who intentionally created you and is available to you every second of your life, no matter how you feel or what you've done. You need that Someone. And so does your daughter.

READ Isaiah 57:15.

What two ways is God described in this passage?

Yes, He is holy and revered—"The High and Exalted One who lives forever, whose name is Holy." But He's also a Shepherd who loves His flock and tends to them—"and [I live] with the oppressed and lowly of spirit, to revive the spirit of the lowly and revive the heart of the oppressed."

Whether you have a cuddly little preschool girl who is toddling around your house or a budding young adult about to leave the nest, it's very important to understand how the culture is influencing her developing heart and mind. We should never underestimate its force, which is like a powerful river that carries everything downstream with it. You can and must help your daughters avoid being swept by the current into unknown waters.

THIS WEEK'S INSIGHTS

• • •

- Culture is bent on scripting what is important and what is beautiful for our daughters.
- We can protect our children from the dangerous current of culture by helping them focus on the message of Jesus.
- We must educate ourselves about who Jesus is.

How can you steer your daughter toward God and away from culture's negative influence?

WRAP UP

• • •

PRAY TOGETHER for wisdom as you continue to consider what it means to bring up godly girls.

Holy God, help us to seek You. Guide us toward a deeper knowledge of You so that our daughters may, by our example, find true value and beauty in You alone. Amen.

READ AND COMPLETE the activities for this section before your next group time. For further insight, read chapters 2 and 14 from *Bringing Up Girls.*

> "The scariest thing about having a daughter is realizing that she will be subjected to a very skewed culture as to what beauty is. I want her to know that her beauty comes from her heart—not her clothes or her appearance."
> **JEFF,** *father of daughter, age 3*

COMBAT CULTURE'S LIES

Scripture calls God's Word a powerful sword. (See Eph. 6:17.) Of all the parts of God's armor, the sword is the only offensive weapon. We need a powerful weapon to ward off the dangerous effects of culture's war for our daughters.

READ Proverbs 31:10-31 as that weapon.

Name two attributes of a Proverbs 31 wife that you found significant.

How has a woman's beauty been distorted by culture?

FOR MOMS: How have you wrestled with and been affected by society's image of what is beautiful?

FOR DADS: Knowing what you know about how men objectify a woman's appearance, how will you help your daughter avoid those traps? Will you have the courage to speak the truth to your daughter? (You may be the only man in her life who will.)

Parents need to be aware of the pressures children face from the culture. The worship of beauty is so pervasive that it influences every dimension of childhood. And it will continue to have an impact throughout her life.

TIME WITH YOUR GIRL

You may already spend hours in the mall with your daughter, but consider using that time to talk through a godly understanding of modesty. Depending on the age of your daughter, you may choose to do several different things. One may include taking your daughter shoe shopping and letting her try on every shoe in the store. Another may be going to a clothing store to try on several stylish dresses. Keep in mind that you don't have to purchase anything during these times, just use the experience to engage her in conversations about modesty.

Use the following passages of Scripture as a model for modesty:

- Psalm 139:13-16
- Proverbs 11:22
- Proverbs 31:30
- Ephesians 2:10

Here are some helpful ideas and activities to keep in mind as you teach your daughter about modesty:

PICKING OUT CLOTHES: Each day, give your toddler or elementary-age daughter two or three options and allow her to choose her outfit. You may even want to create an "Anything Day," letting her choose anything she wants in any combination to wear for the day. A middle school girl may be completely in charge of what she wears as long as you maintain control of what is bought. As long as parents are aware of what goes in a closet, it's safe to give a teen daughter freedom to choose her wardrobe. High school girls can be in charge of their own shopping as long as parents maintain open communication and remind their daughters that questionable purchases can be returned.

ENCOURAGEMENT: Be aware of negative body-image comments and how you're responding to this kind of talk. Kids (even at young ages) can learn to calmly articulate their feelings as well as the things they would like to change about themselves. Think about creating a sentence that your daughter can use when discussing her image.

"I feel like _____ about my _____."
"I would like to change my _____ because ..."

TEACHABLE MOMENTS: Use teachable moments to talk with your daughter about culture's attacks on modesty. This may happen while watching a TV show you're not comfortable with. Instead of slamming down the rule book without an explanation, take time to talk through your thoughts on the show and what is portrayed. Ask her questions. Maybe you're at the mall and see an inappropriate outfit; use that time to discuss why that outfit may not be exemplary of a godly woman, all the while elevating the values of modesty and purity.

ATTITUDE OF OPENNESS: Make sure as a parent you're open and available for discussion. Your daughter needs to know she can ask you anything. Don't jump to conclusions because she is asking these questions. If you say, "no," depending on her age, she also needs to understand the reason behind the no. Cultivate a relationship of trust so she understands your response is in her best interests.

HEALTHY LIVING: Frequently talk about the importance of eating healthy and exercise over the importance of outward appearance. Commit as a family to these things, communicating the value of both. And don't demean your own appearance or that of other family members.

CULTIVATE A RELATIONSHIP

If we're not careful, culture can creep in and turn our hearts from God.

Where does your repeated exposure to the lure of culture take place? In the checkout line? On the Internet? In front of the TV? Where do you find you or your daughter growing deeply attached to something you know isn't productive or healthy?

An emphasis on sex is prevalent in our culture. However, with parental help, girls can understand why morality and modesty are important. These are priceless gifts that your girl gives herself. Cultivate a relationship with your daughters to communicate truth to them daily. The earlier you get started, the better.

> **How can you cultivate a relationship with your daughter that helps to distract her repeated exposure to culture?**

Dr. Robert Blum, professor and chair of the Department of Population, Family, and Reproductive Health at Johns Hopkins University, published a study designed to gauge parental influences on a girl's sexual behavior. His overall conclusion? The quality of the relationship between teens and their mothers was the primary factor in support of virginity.[2] When the girls felt close to their moms and were aware that they disapproved of premarital sex, they were less likely to engage in such activities. Parental closeness was pivotal, but it resulted less from family activities and "lectures" than it did from parents' regular involvement in their children's lives.

This doesn't give the father a free pass. A number of other studies reveal that older teenage girls who have better relationships with their fathers tend to postpone sexual activity longer. Researchers conclude that those who are close to their fathers tend to have fewer boyfriends, feel more guilty about having premarital sex, and tend to eat more meals together with their families.

In short, having a healthy relationship with your daughter helps to inoculate her against immoral behavior. In a world where thousands of American teenagers contract venereal disease every day, that is very good news.[3] Unfortunately, mothers and fathers are often unaware of their impact.

PERSONAL REFLECTION

Consider this passage:

> If we say, "We have no sin," we are deceiving ourselves,
> and the truth is not in us. If we confess our sins,
> He is faithful and righteous to forgive us our sins
> and to cleanse us from all unrighteousness.
> **1 JOHN 1:8-9**

Spend time asking God to help you be honest as you reflect on the following questions. Ask for insight into your heart's desires and practices and God's help to overcome the influence of culture in them.

What in your life needs to be confessed and repented of because of repeated exposure to culture? How could you encourage your daughter to do the same?

This week, what's one way you are going to help cultivate a relationship with your daughter?

1. Vicki Courtney, *Your Girl: Raising a Godly Daughter in an Ungodly World* (Nashville: B&H Publishing Group, 2012), 10-11.
2. Christine C. Kim, "Teen Sex: The Parent Factor," *Backgrounder*, Heritage Foundation, no. 2194 (October 7, 2008).
3. "2010 Sexually Transmitted Diseases Surveillance," Centers for Disease Control and Prevention (online), 17 November 2011 [cited 11 July 2013]. Available from the Internet: *www.cdc.gov/std/stats10/trends.htm.*

WEEK 3
THE THREE Ts
TALK
· · · · · · · · · · · ·
TOUCH
· · · · · · · · · · · ·
& TIME
· · · · · · · · · · · ·

START YOUR GROUP TIME by discussing what participants discovered in their Reflect homework.

Answer the following questions with your group. Be aware that some of your conversations may bring up painful memories. Be sensitive to participants who may be reluctant to share.

Like it or not, much of our parenting comes from how we were parented.

> Which one of the following statements describes you?
> ☐ I can only hope to raise my child as well as my parents raised me.
> ☐ I hope to avoid most of the mistakes my parents made along the way.
>
> In what ways did your family show love well? How did your family miss at this?
>
> How well did you connect with your mom? Your dad?
>
> What are the relationship-building parts of your family of origin you hope to pass on to your kids? What do you hope to avoid?

If you didn't grow up in a nurturing, loving environment, all is not lost. While it may prove challenging to parent in a way that was not modeled for you, you have something working in your favor: God's power. As with any calling, He equips us for tasks we're not prepared to tackle. He doesn't demand perfection or even pure motivation in the process. He's simply looking for a contrite heart and a willingness to be obedient. "For it is God who is working in you, enabling you both to desire and work out His good purpose" (Phil. 2:13).

Again, be aware of what you are modeling to your girl about God: demanding taskmaster or grace-filled encourager?

WATCH CLIP 3 from the study DVD and answer the following questions:

Rate your family of origin and your current family on the following scales. For *family of origin*, circle the rating. For your *current family*, draw a box around your rating.

TALK:

1	2	3	4	5	6	7	8	9	10

Secretive   Open

TOUCH:

1	2	3	4	5	6	7	8	9	10

Cold   Warm

TIME:

1	2	3	4	5	6	7	8	9	10

Scarce   Abundant

Talk about the continuum above. Give illustrations from your family of origin.

Which T does your family struggle with the most?

Which do you personally struggle with the most? Why?

Which T do you think your daughter desires most?

● **CONTINUE YOUR GROUP TIME** with this discussion guide.

There is no Bible verse that demands, "Parents, talk to your kids!" Nor are there verses that explain the biblically rooted values of appropriate touch and quality time. In fact, all of the parenting stories in the Bible tell of sinful people and their flawed kids (excluding one Savior). Even Adam and Eve, first in the perfect garden, sinned and had broken children. So, with that in mind, consider the benefits of pouring the Three Ts into your kids and see what happens.

Let's start with *talking*. This kind of talk is not about rules and regulations—those belong in other discussions; instead, this kind of talk involves conversations about your daughter's hopes, needs, hurts, failings, fears, and dreams.

● **READ** Matthew 15:21-28 and discuss the encounter and conversation between Jesus and the Gentile woman.

Notice her persistence. This mom was not taking no for an answer. The life of her daughter was at stake.

How would your daughter describe you regarding talk? How approachable would she say that you are?

How persistent is your daughter for talk time with you? How persistent are you with her?

What impediments keep you from meaningful times of conversation?

How was the woman's persistence an illustration of great faith? What could you learn from her?

READ Matthew 8:1-3.

Leviticus 13 prescribed that people with skin diseases couldn't be touched. They were to be pronounced unclean and cast out from the community to live alone.

Jesus healed this man in two ways. How?

What good things does physical touch communicate? How has physical touch been a healing agent in your life?

Considering ways that physical touch is part of your parenting. You'll be encouraged to evaluate all of the Three Ts this week during the Reflect section.

READ Luke 19:5-10.

What about the Zacchaeus encounter resonates with you?

The encounter with Jesus changed everything about Zacchaeus. The pattern and trajectory of his life were forever altered by this moment with Christ.

We have far more time with our daughters than Jesus had with Zacchaeus. As we invest this time in our daughters lives we would likely say they're a good investment of our time. But do our actions support our words?

COMPLETE this survey and discuss your observations with the group.

___ Number of hours you spend each day watching TV

___ Number of non-work-related hours you spend each day on the Internet

___ Number of times per week you eat together as a family

___ Number of times per week you pray as a family

___ Number of hours your child spends in extracurricular activities each week

___ Number of hours you spend each week on leisure activities

___ Number of hours each day your child spends alone

This is not a guilt trip: it's an awareness journey. It's not possible to spend hours every day with your daughter, but how could you be more intentional with the time you spend with her? Do your best to spare your girl of the ever-present "how-was-your-day" question. Instead tell her about something in your day that reminded you of her—"I saw a picture of the Eiffel Tower and it reminded me of you and your curiosity about Paris." Or ask her about her happiest thing that day. Or saddest.

THIS WEEK'S INSIGHTS

• • •

- Your children need your presence. More than your money and your provision, they need time with you.
- Your children need to feel love, tenderness, and encouragement through your words and appropriate physical affection.
- The goal of parenting is to encourage your children to seek God. The investment you make has significant eternal implications.

What is your plan of action for incorporating the Three Ts in your parenting?

What are you doing well in these areas? How can you continue your efforts?

If you are struggling in any of these areas, in what ways do you plan to start fresh?

WRAP UP

• • •

PRAY TOGETHER thanking God for His continued presence in your lives.

> Father, thank You for always being there to listen to us and guide us. Thank You for Your ever-present forgiving and healing touch in our lives. Thank You for never growing tired or weary. Thank You for Your Word and Your voice. We know that our daughters' initial understanding of You comes from us. As You shape us, allow the reality of You in our lives shape them. Amen.

● **READ AND COMPLETE** the activities for this section before your next group time. For further insight, read chapters 7 and 9 in the book *Bringing Up Girls.*

> "The best thing about raising a girl for me is the connection and responsibility I have in raising her as a child of God. It is amazing to see how intuitive my daughter is, and how her nurturing and merciful spirit blesses others. There is a special connection a mom and daughter can share because of the opportunity to mentor and be a healthy role model for her . . . and then hopefully, she [will mentor] another."
> **SHANNON,** *mother of daughter, age 5*

GROWING UP

Take a moment to look at female development to better understand what her body does and how to respond.

One of the earliest stages of development is called juvenile puberty— a period of estrogen saturation that begins in girls between six and thirty months of age. Along with others, this hormone wires the brain for femininity and prepares it for all that will come afterward. When she's three years of age, estrogen levels fall dramatically, and a period of relative quiet occurs hormonally. This is called the juvenile pause, and it lasts for five to eight years.[1] During that period, girls are typically disinterested in boys and don't even like them very much. The feeling is often mutual.

Immediately after the juvenile pause, puberty comes on like a house afire. The girl enters a period of intense physical, emotional, and neurological transformation. The timing of this new phase is genetically controlled, although it also appears to be affected by family stability and other factors such as weight gain.[2] Ultimately, however, puberty is set into motion by signals from the hypothalamus.[3] Massive amounts of estrogen are produced, marinating her brain a second time, which begins to spur maturation and sexual development. Three other primary hormones are involved in puberty: progesterone, testosterone, and growth hormones.[4] When they work in concert, it's like fireworks on the Fourth of July.

> **What are the challenges you've faced or think you may face when your daughter hits puberty?**

Parents should understand that the hormonal barrage that initiates puberty is highly traumatic to the female brain, and it can throw a girl into complete disequilibrium until she begins to adjust to it.[5] During this stage, your daughter may give you the impression that she doesn't need your talk, touch, and time—but she does. But be sensitive to what she is going through. Her emotions are on a roller coaster; help her hang on for dear life.

PRESS IN

READ Matthew 7:7-11

Let's examine two perspectives from this passage:

1. God is our Heavenly Father and we can seek more of Him and be blessed as a result.
2. God is our example of what a good father (parent) is like in blessing children with good and not evil.

> **What's your reaction to these perspectives? Why?**

> **What do your children need most from you?**

Jesus instructs us to press in and be bold as we ask for what we need from God. God's response is to give us His Spirit, a measure of Himself. Your children don't need stuff as much as they need you. They need your presence, your touch, and your time. They need your words of encouragement.

TIME WITH YOUR GIRL

Creating small traditions for your daughter shows that you cherish being with her. It doesn't have to be brilliant or grand; just intentional.

Locate a spot in your home you'll see often, and write down the name of your daughter. Form a game plan for giving her individual time, touch, and talk on a regular basis. Make it easy and simple so you'll follow through. Choose things you both enjoy. Include activities you already do together.

Activity	Time allotted	Frequency
1.		
2.		
3.		

It may feel silly to formally write a commitment to hug your daughter or spend one-on-one time eating with her, playing with her, or talking to her. But your relationship with each of your children will be blessed by making and keeping these commitments. Not only that, your family as a whole will be forever shaped by how you commit to the Three Ts.

CONVERSATIONS WITH YOUR GIRL

Here are six tips to generate good conversations with your girl:

1. **READ TO YOUR DAUGHTER.** Before she can even talk, she'll know how wonderful words really are.

2. **EXPRESS HONOR AND RESPECT IN CONVERSATION.** Don't let her interrupt you. And don't interrupt her. Model for her the right ways to enter a conversation and also the importance of patiently waiting for her turn.

3. **LET HER TAG ALONG ON YOUR ERRANDS.** Take her with you. Make car time valuable by talking along the way. Play car games like I Spy, Punch Bug, and Count the Cows.

4. **ASK GOOD QUESTIONS.** Use subjective and open-ended questions that keep her thinking and talking.

5. **TEACH HER MANNERS.** Show her how to meet someone new and greet a friend, especially other adults.

6. **APOLOGIZE WHEN YOU MESS UP.** Not only do you show care for her as a person, but you also model what it means to admit your faults. This will be very important for her as she experiences Christ, deals with relationships, and communicates in a marriage one day.[6]

> Make a list of the most important conversations your parents had with you. Were they about Jesus? Sexuality? Manners? Driving safety?

Make a second list of topics to discuss with your daughter. Include an age next to each topic, indicating when you hope to have that conversation with her.

PERSONAL REFLECTION

• • •

This week, ask God for more Holy Spirit in your life. Luke 11:13 asks, "How much more will the heavenly Father give the Holy Spirit to those who ask Him?" Be persistent in your asking and hopeful in your expectation. It's an illustration of faith in God to ask Him for what you need rather than attempting to go it alone. You need the presence of the Holy Spirit to parent your children.

In what areas of parenting are you experiencing the Spirit's presence? In what areas are you going solo?

How is that working out for you? What should you do about this?

---

1. Ron G. Rosenfeld and Barbara C. Nicodemus, "The Transition from Adolescence to Adult Life: Physiology of the 'Transition' Phase and Its Evolutionary Basis,' GHD during Critical Phases of Life, 6th KIGS/KIMS Expert Meeting on Growth Hormone and Growth Disorders, Florence, Italy (November 8-9, 2002).
2. Ibid.
3. Alecia D. Schweinsburg, Bonnnie J. Nagel, et al., "fMRI Reveals Alteration of Spatial Working Memory Networks across Adolescence," *Journal of International Neuropsychological Society* 11, no. 5 (2005): 631-644.
4. Michael Gurian, Ph.D., *The Wonder of Girls* (New York: Simon and Schuster, 2002), 75.
5. Louann Brizendine, *The Female Brain* (New York: Morgan Road Books, 2006), 12.
6. Adapted from *She Calls Me Daddy* by Robert Wolgemuth, (Carol Stream, IL: Tyndale House Publishers, 1999), 77-78.

WEEK 4

GENERATIONAL
IMPACT

START YOUR GROUP TIME by discussing what participants discovered in their Reflect homework.

How old will your daughter be ten years from now? Discuss the qualities you want her to embody at that age. What about twenty years from now?

How would you like for your adult daughter to remember and reflect on the following:

1. Her childhood

2. Your parenting

3. Your family dynamic

4. The Three Ts in your home

Let's think about those answers for a moment. Those are our goals. Parenting with the end in mind means making decisions every day to ensure that she grows up with those thoughts, feelings, and memories. The way our adult daughters regard us and the life they lived under our care will be the result of decisions we are making right now.

Turn to page 17 of the first session and revisit the mission statement you made for your daughter. This statement is parenting with the end in mind. Rewrite that statement now.

These statements are the start of parenting toward an achievable goal—and understanding how important each moment of each day is in terms of shaping the woman your girl will become.

WATCH CLIP 4 from the study DVD and answer the following questions:

In this clip, my daughter, Danae, and I share stage time and memories of life together as father and daughter. What we share is a simple recipe for spending significant time together and the impact that lifestyle can make.

Based on what you saw, how would you describe the relationship between Danae and me?

Do you think that similar positive outcomes are a possibility for you and your relationship with your daughter? Why or why not?

What did you notice about our talk that you might incorporate into your life with your daughter?

CONTINUE YOUR GROUP TIME with this discussion guide.

God's Word includes quite a few examples of generational impact. A quick scan of Old Testament history reveals both positive and negative examples. The phrases "good in God's sight just as his father had done," and "evil in God's sight just as his father had done" are repeated throughout 1 and 2 Kings, referencing all of Israel's and Judah's senior leaders.

In the New Testament, one of the best examples we have is Timothy.

READ Acts 16:1-3 and 2 Timothy 1:3-6.

What motivated Paul to disciple Timothy?

Who helped disciple you? What did they do to steer you toward the gospel and growth in Jesus?

Paul was responsible for leading Timothy to Christ during his first missionary journey. When he returned on his second journey, he invited Timothy to come with him. Timothy's father was a Gentile, but his mother and grandmother were God-fearing Jews who also trusted Jesus as Savior.

READ 1 Corinthians 4:15-17.

What does this passage reveal about the pattern for generational impact according to Paul?

Paul was very much a spiritual father to Timothy in way he modeled his life and ministry for Timothy. And we see this pattern of modeling and imitating throughout Paul's letter. Paul sent Timothy to the church in Corinth to remind them about Paul's ways in Jesus Christ. Later on in 1 Corinthians, Paul instructed the church to imitate him as he imitates Christ. (See 1 Cor. 11:1.)

> Who do you look to today to be a better Christ follower? Husband? Wife? Parent?

> If your daughter imitates you, is she then imitating Christ? Reflect on that question for a moment.

> What about your daily life needs realignment so that this truth will be evident in your life and in your daughter's life?

Perhaps this part of the study is discouraging. Our daughters may not be spiritually where we'd hoped. Maybe we did everything we knew to do and things have somehow ended up wrong. Take comfort in the fact that our effort will not return void. Be steadfast in your love and guidance. The story is not over. God is still at work. Remain faithful.

READ 1 Corinthians 15:58 and 1 Corinthians 3:5-7.

Before we get too puffed up with pride over the godly girls we've raised or too discouraged over a rebellious daughter, take note of Paul's words to the Corinthians in chapter 3. We can invest everything we have. We can hug them until our arms grow weak. We can quit our jobs and spend every moment of every day loving them and showing them Jesus. But remember, it's God who produces growth.

The reality of the situation is that it all depends on Him—and that should comfort us. Jesus told us that He would carry our burdens. As much as parenting is a joy, it's also a big responsibility. He wants to do it for us and through us.

If it's true that children should be trained in the knowledge of the Lord, and Scripture tells us it is, then there is one task in parenting that outranks all others in significance. It's the responsibility of Christian mothers and fathers to introduce their children to Jesus Christ and to cultivate their understanding of Him at every opportunity. The apostle Paul established this priority when he wrote, "Don't stir up anger in your children, but bring them up in the training and instruction of the Lord" (Eph. 6:4).

> Think about times you've introduced your girl to Jesus and cultivated her understanding of Him. What kinds of success did you find during those times?

> What kinds of resistance or disappointments did you experience?

People don't care how much we know until they know how much we care. Think about the video clip. It was about bike rides, tape recorders, Cinderella songs, sandcastles, swing sets, and ice cream—hardly anyone's go-to recipe for spiritual growth, right? Or is it? Let's consider the time we spend with our daughter playing board games and dress-up as opportunities to become her friend. Think of sleepless nights with her crying over a bully or a boy as a chance to earn her trust. Think of family vacations and days at the park as ways to guide her heart.

All of these seemingly insignificant moments are the ones your daughter will treasure. Relationships are the best context for evangelism and discipleship. If we want to reach and teach our daughters, find time to play games with them first. Carefully listen to them—their words and their heart.

THIS WEEK'S INSIGHTS

- You are to follow Christ first, so that as your daughter follows you, she follows Jesus too. Your children cannot see and follow Jesus if you aren't heading in His direction.
- The Three Ts and all other things you do to develop a relationship with your daughter give you ground to speak spiritual truth into her life.
- The goal is to foster a special relationship your daughter will always remember. The little things are the ways you build and keep her trust and her love. They are evidence of parenting with the end in mind.

In what way(s) can you teach these important truths to your daughter this week?

In what way(s) can you better steer her toward Jesus this week?

WRAP UP

PRAY TOGETHER as you close this session.

Holy God, the most important thing we do in our
daughters' lives is pointing them toward Your Son.
May they cling to hope in Christ. Make us better
followers of Your Son so that they will in turn do
the same. Help us to show them Your presence
in our lives in all we say and do. Amen.

● **READ AND COMPLETE** the activities for this section before your next group time. For further insight, read chapters 5 and 12 in the book *Bringing Up Girls.*

> "The scariest thing about having a daughter is the inevitability that she will be confronted by the cruelties of a world that is growing ever darker. As I watch her parent my granddaughters now, I can only pray for God to cover and protect them as they navigate this world's challenges, particularly with regard to technological advances, that when used for anything other than good may invite torment, temptation, and taunting that my generation never faced."
> **SANDY**, *Nana to 3 granddaughters*

SIX PARENTAL BEHAVIORS

Creating a generational impact starts with how you are interacting with your daughter on a daily basis. Frank Luntz offers six additional steps parents can take to help foster this relationship.

1. **HAVE DINNER WITH YOUR CHILDREN.** If you spend at least five nights a week having dinner as a family, you show your children that they are a high priority to you. Not having dinner with your children gives the opposite message, which is heard loud and clear.

2. **TAKE YOUR CHILDREN TO CHURCH.** The most successful anti-drug and anti-alcohol programs have a spiritual component. If children are shown the importance of having a relationship with Christ, they are more likely to appreciate their life and less likely to destroy it with drugs and alcohol.

3. **CHECK YOUR CHILD'S HOMEWORK NIGHTLY.** Parents' attentiveness to and participation in their child's education communicates that their children matter. Another benefit: checking homework reveals if your child needs help in certain areas.

4. **EMPHASIZE THE BENEFIT OF TRUTH.** Parents need to communicate that truth brings relief and insight. Encourage your kids to be truthful not only to you, but to themselves as well. Explain that it is hard to tell the truth; that's why a person who can speak truth has a priceless asset in life. Truth plays out in boundaries: not every place, friend, or behavior is acceptable. Promote honesty in their thoughts, words, and deeds in relaying their activities. Point out that lies always snowball, leading to internal guilt and external trouble.

5. **TAKE YOUR FAMILY ON VACATION FOR AT LEAST A WEEK AT A TIME.** Weekend vacations just won't do. You need something to break the daily routine to reconnect relationships. A week without phones or computers will draw a family together.

6. **ENCOURAGE THEM TO PARTICIPATE IN A TEAM SPORT.** When teens are forced to depend on each other in physical competition, they are less likely to engage in harmful behaviors. Peer pressure for good can be a powerful motivating force.[1]

YOUR GREATEST FEAR

READ Judges 2:10-13.

You likely have many fears as a parent. None of them, however, is as dangerous as life without Christ.

In Judges 2, we see God's people beginning to unravel again. The next generation wasn't faithful like the one before it. It wasn't just that they did wrong; Judges 2:10 says they didn't know the Lord or the works He had done for them.

> Whose responsibility was it to teach them, and where did the breakdown occur?

SPIRITUAL GROWTH PLAN

Have you developed a spiritual growth plan for your daughter? Consider the following ideas as you make your own map for growth.

PRESCHOOL DAUGHTERS: Find a storybook Bible and read it to your daughter before bed. Put her name on it and call it her Bible. Enjoy the colors and pictures. Help her get acquainted with key Bible characters and stories. Remind her that these may be cartoon pictures, but that these were real people who lived a long time ago. She needs to know that those people are real and, more important, that God is real. Focus on the love of God—His protection, His encouragement, His creation, His gifts to us.

ELEMENTARY SCHOOL-AGE DAUGHTERS: Continue daily Bible reading as you graduate to a copy of the Scripture. Again, put her name on it. Call it her Bible. Pick up a children's devotional guide or use Sunday School curriculum as supplemental material. Spend time on the adventure found in God—read about specific women in the Bible, showing their good and wayward choices. Check out books on female missionaries and martyrs.

PRETEENS AND TEENS: Make sure your older daughter has an age-appropriate study Bible. Put her name on it. Develop a daily routine in which she has her own "turned off and tuned out" time. No media. No friends. No phone. Just a few moments of quiet each day to encounter God. Give her a prayer journal to record her private thoughts, prayers, and experiences. Encourage her to give back to the church through helping with childcare, teaching younger students, or researching mission projects she'd like to be involved in. Go on a mission trip with her.

READ Joel 1:3.

This is the goal. We want our children to grow up with faith and then lead their children to do the same.

FAITH PLAN

Which of the following elements will you emphasize in guiding your daughter to a fuller understanding of the gospel?

☐ Bible reading and memorization
☐ Church participation
☐ Missions (local, national, and international)
☐ Serving others
☐ Daily prayers
☐ Lifestyle worship

READ AND CONSIDER these passages of Scripture:

☐ Psalm 34:11
☐ Psalm 78:4,6
☐ Psalm 119:11
☐ Psalm 145:4
☐ Ephesians 6:4

What do each of these verses tell us about parents raising kids to know and follow God?

What other passages of Scripture stand out to you and impact your walk as a parent?

In a George Barna nationwide poll, results showed that children ages 5 through 13 have a 32 percent probability of accepting Jesus Christ as their Savior. That rate drops dramatically to just 4 percent for kids age 14 to 18. And those who have not become Christians before age 19 have only a 6 percent probability of doing so during the rest of their lives. There is no time to lose.[2]

Pray for the salvation of your daughter. Remember to approach the throne of God with boldness (see Heb. 4:16), as a child approaches her generous parent with eagerness in her request. So be bold. Ask for the amazing. Be alert to where God is working in her life by asking her questions about her day. Her friends. Her dreams.

Also remember you're praying for an ongoing relationship with Christ that will shape your daughter's direction, desires, and decisions. If she has already accepted Jesus as her Savior, pray for continued growth, revelation, and fellowship. And pray for yourself—that you won't hinder her growth by your own fears, including the fear of her walk not looking like yours.

PERSONAL REFLECTION

Use additional paper if necessary to compose a prayer for your daughter. You could include parts of Jesus' prayer for believers (see John 17) or some of the passages of Scripture you have encountered during this study. Plan also to include the mission statement you created for her.

Whether you share the prayer with her is up to you—it's more an outlined spiritual statement for you than her. Refer to it as you continually seek God for His wisdom, direction, and blessing in bringing up a godly girl who knows and follows Him well.

1. Adapted from *What Americans Want ... Really: The Truth about Our Hopes, Dreams, and Fears* by Frank Luntz, Hyperion, 2009.
2. John W. Kennedy, "The 4-14 Window," *Christianity Today* (online), July 2004 [cited 27 May 2014]. Available from the Internet: *www.christianitytoday.com/ct/2004/july/37.53.html.*

Key Insights

WEEK 1

- Our daughters are unique. Their femininity is a special part of creation that bears the image of God.
- Our daughters' deepest desire is to know that they are loved and are lovely.
- There is a war going on for the rights to our daughters' hearts. God wants to restore His image in her life through the life and likeness of His Son. The world wants to tell her that her worth is found in possessions, looks, and others' opinions.

WEEK 2

- Culture is bent on scripting what is important and what is beautiful for our daughters.
- We can protect our children from the dangerous current of culture by helping them focus on the message of Jesus.
- We must educate ourselves about who Jesus truly is.

WEEK 3

- Your children need your presence. More than your money and your provision, they need time with you.
- Your children need to feel love, tenderness, and encouragement through your words and appropriate physical affection.
- The goal of parenting is to encourage your children to seek God. The investment you make has significant eternal implications.

WEEK 4

- You are to follow Christ first so that as your children follow you, they follow Jesus too. Your children cannot see and follow Jesus if you aren't heading in His direction.
- The Three Ts and all other things you do to develop a relationship with your daughter give you ground to speak spiritual truth into her life.
- The goal is to foster a special relationship your daughter will always remember. The little things are the ways you build and keep her trust and her love. They are evidence of parenting with the end in mind.

Leader Notes

It's time for a leadership adventure. Don't worry; you don't have to have all the answers. Your role is to facilitate the group discussion, getting participants back on topic when they stray, encouraging everyone to share honestly and authentically, and guiding those who might dominate the conversation to make sure others are also getting some time to share.

As facilitator, take time to look over this entire study guide, noting the order and requirements of each session. Watch all the videos as well. Take time to read the suggested chapters (noted in the beginning of each Reflect section) from the book *Bringing Up Girls* (ISBN 978-1-4143-9132-8). And pray over the material, the prospective participants, and your time together.

You have the option of extending your group's study by showing the films *Bringing Up Girls* and *Your Legacy*. You can also keep it to four weeks by using just this study guide and DVD. The study is easy to customize for your group's needs.

Go over the "How to Use This Study" and the "Guidelines for Groups" sections with participants, making everyone aware of best practices and the steps of each session. Then dive into Week 1.

In establishing a schedule for each group meeting, consider ordering these elements for the hour of time together:

> 1. Connect—10 minutes
> 2. Watch—15 minutes
> 3. Engage—35 minutes

Be sure to allow time during each session to show the video clip. All four clips are approximately eight minutes or less in length. Reflect refers to the home study or activities done between group sessions.

Beginning with session 2, encourage some sharing regarding the previous week's Reflect home study. Usually at least one Connect question allows for this interaction. Sharing about the previous week's activities encourages participants to study on their own and be ready to share with their group during the next session.

As the study comes to a close, consider some ways to keep in touch. There may be some additional studies for which group members would like information. Some may be interested in knowing more about your church.

Occasionally, a group member may have needs that fall outside the realm of a supportive small group. If someone would be better served by the pastoral staff at your church or a professional counselor, please gather a list of professionals to privately offer to that person, placing his/her road to recovery in the hands of a qualified pastor or counselor.

Use the space below to make notes or to identify specific page numbers and questions you would like to discuss with your small group each week based on their needs and season of life.

Further Resources

Need more guidance? Check out the following for help.

ON PARENTING:

The New Dare to Discipline by Dr. James Dobson

The New Strong-Willed Child by Dr. James Dobson

Bringing Up Boys by Dr. James Dobson

Bringing Up Girls by Dr. James Dobson

Dr. Dobson's Handbook of Family Advice by Dr. James Dobson

Night Light for Parents by Dr. James Dobson

Parenting Isn't for Cowards by Dr. James Dobson

Raising Boys and Girls by Sissy Goff, David Thomas, and Melissa Trevathan

Love No Matter What by Brenda Garrison

Intentional Parenting by Sissy Goff, David Thomas, and Melissa Trevathan

Raising Girls by Melissa Trevathan and Sissy Goff

The Back Door to Your Teen's Heart by Melissa Trevathan

5 Love Languages by Gary Chapman

5 Conversations You Must Have with Your Daughter by Vicki Courtney

Parenting Teens magazine

HomeLife magazine

ParentLife magazine

The Parent Adventure by Selma and Rodney Wilson

Experiencing God at Home by Richard Blackaby and Tom Blackaby

Love Dare for Parents by Stephen Kendrick and Alex Kendrick

Authentic Parenting in a Postmodern Culture by Mary E. DeMuth

Grace-Based Parenting by Tim Kimmel

ON DISCUSSING FAITH WITH YOUR CHILDREN:

Bringing the Gospel Home by Randy Newman

Firsthand by Ryan Shook and Josh Shook

God Distorted by John Bishop

Sticky Faith by Dr. Kara E. Powell and Dr. Chap Clark

Parenting Beyond Your Capacity by Reggie Joiner and Carey Nieuwhof

A Praying Life by Paul Miller

Faith Conversations for Families by Jim Burns

Introducing Your Child to Christ

Your most significant calling and privilege as a parent is to introduce your children to Jesus Christ. A good way to begin this conversation is to tell them about your own faith journey.

Outlined below is a simple gospel presentation you can share with your child. Define any terms they don't understand and make it more conversational, letting the Spirit guide your words and allowing your child to ask questions and contribute along the way.

GOD RULES. The Bible tells us God created everything, and He's in charge of everything. (See Gen. 1:1; Col. 1:16-17; Rev. 4:11.)

WE SINNED. We all choose to disobey God. The Bible calls this sin. Sin separates us from God and deserves God's punishment of death. (See Rom. 3:23; 6:23.)

GOD PROVIDED. God sent Jesus, the perfect solution to our sin problem, to rescue us from the punishment we deserve. It's something we, as sinners, could never earn on our own. Jesus alone saves us. (See John 3:16; Eph. 2:8-9.)

JESUS GIVES. He lived a perfect life, died on the cross for our sins, and rose again. Because Jesus gave up His life for us, we can be welcomed into God's family for eternity. This is the best gift ever! (See Rom. 5:8; 2 Cor. 5:21; Eph. 2:8-9; 1 Pet. 3:18.)

WE RESPOND. Believe in your heart that Jesus alone saves you through what He's already done on the cross. Repent, by turning away from your sin. Tell God and others that your faith is in Jesus. (See John 14:6; Rom. 10:9-10,13.)

If your child is ready to respond, explain what it means for Jesus to be Lord of his or her life. Guide your child to a time in prayer to repent and express his or her belief in Jesus. If your child responds in faith, celebrate! You now have the opportunity to disciple your child to be more like Christ.

BUILD YOUR FAMILY LEGACY.

Dr. James Dobson leads you through his classic messages and new insights for today's families in these eight DVD-based Bible studies. Each Building a Family Legacy Bible study includes four-sessions with personal reflection and discussion guides along with a DVD of Dr. Dobson's teachings, introduced by his son, Ryan. Studies include:

Your Legacy Bible Study
Bringing Up Boys Bible Study
Bringing Up Girls Bible Study
Dare to Discipline Bible Study
The Strong-Willed Child Bible Study
Straight Talk to Men Bible Study
Love for a Lifetime Bible Study
Wanting to Believe Bible Study

Learn more at LifeWay.com/Legacy

DR. JAMES DOBSON **BUILDING A FAMILY LEGACY**™

Dr. James Dobson's **BUILDING A FAMILY LEGACY** campaign includes films, Bible studies, and books designed to help families of all ages and stages. Dr. Dobson's wisdom, insight, and humor promise to strengthen marriages and help parents meet the remarkable challenges of raising children. Most importantly, **BUILDING A FAMILY LEGACY** will inspire parents to lead their children to personal faith in Jesus Christ.

Learn more at

BUILDINGAFAMILYLEGACY.COM

BUILDING A FAMILY LEGACY BOOKS

From Dr. James Dobson and Tyndale Momentum

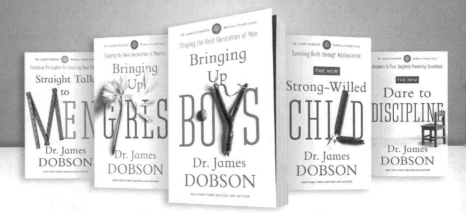

BRINGING UP BOYS • 978-1-4143-9133-5
Also available in hardcover (978-0-8423-5266-6) and audio CDs
(978-0-8423-2297-3)

BRINGING UP GIRLS • 978-1-4143-9132-8
Also available in hardcover (978-1-4143-0127-3) and audio CDs
read by Dr. James Dobson (978-1-4143-3650-3)

THE NEW STRONG-WILLED CHILD • 978-1-4143-9134-2
Also available in hardcover (978-0-8423-3622-2) and audio
CDs (978-0-8423-8799-6), as well as *The New Strong-Willed
Child Workbook* (978-1-4143-0382-6)

THE NEW DARE TO DISCIPLINE • 978-1-4143-9135-9

STRAIGHT TALK TO MEN • 978-1-4143-9131-1

AVAILABLE IN 2015

LOVE FOR A LIFETIME
Revised and expanded edition
978-1-4964-0328-5